The Greatest Facts
in the
History of Facts

by the editors of Klutz

KLUTZ®

Table of Contents

Introduction

The facts in this book have been thoroughly checked against multiple sources — then double checked, triple checked, and reviewed by Dr. Paul Doherty, our trusted and long-suffering science advisor. However, Paul would like to add a word that bears not just on this book, but on the World in general.

Paul says: "It's more complicated than that."

Paul is referring to the Truth, which is — always and inevitably — more complicated than any telling of it will ever be. All truth is partial truth. No important fact is entirely 100% true when you examine it at every level and from every point of view.

But this is all good news! A universe in which something was certain without doubt, nuance, or contradiction would be a universe that had nobody in it who could look around and describe it from their unique (and limited) point of view. And who wants to live in a universe like that?

FACT

This is a book of facts but there were, of course, some non-fact opinions involved in its creation. Take the title, for example. Some may dispute that these are the "greatest" facts. After all, we came to the conclusion that these facts were the greatest through a process many scientists would call "arbitrary." "By what criteria," they might ask, "are these the 'greatest facts in the history of facts'?"

We welcome this question because we actually know the answer. Our answer is: "Who knows? We just decided." That's what arbitrary is all about. Our opinions are our own and we support them without apology or, occasionally, support. Sometimes we just feel things, and that's that.

And we feel that these facts will stretch your brain, stagger your imagination, and amaze your friends. All that strikes us as rather great.

— the editors of Klutz

You Are Very Unlikely

When we began reviewing all the facts out there with the goal of selecting the greatest, we were pretty excited. Big projects do that for us. But we did harbor a nagging concern about one fact, the first one. It's a lonely spot up there at the top.

It didn't help that everybody who heard about the project had the same annoying question: "What's The Number One Fact of All Time?"

Fortunately, with only a few months to go, a little girl asked us the usual question and the obvious finally came into focus. The Number One Fact of All Time turns out to be the easiest call of all: It's you, gentle reader.

Forget for a second how unlikely it was that your own parents were born, met, and gave birth to you. Let's ask the next question: How many unique individuals can come from the pairing of a particular two human beings? In other words, how many different ways are there to shuffle your parent's genetics?

What are the odds that your parents would have someone just like you? Not good. Not good at all.

Each person has around 30,000 genes, which influence things like the person's height and hair color and allergies and a lot of other characteristics. Each gene comes in a number of forms. No one can tell us exactly how many ways all those genes can be put together, but everyone in the know agrees that it's in the trillions. Which is a lot, given that there are only around 7 billion people on the planet.

There are so many possible combinations of genes that the scientists who study this stuff say that every person has a unique collection of genes. Even identical twins have hundreds of minor differences in their genes.

Think of it this way: You'd be far more likely to win the Mega Millions Jackpot than to get born from your parents. You were, in other words, born a Very Big Winner. Now **that's** a top fact. Congratulations, you unlikely creature you!

Einstein's Brain Is a Celebrity

Albert Einstein was a celebrity in his day. And, though the genius scientist has been understandably inactive since his death in 1955, his brain continues to surprise and impress us. It even has its own Wikipedia page.

After Einstein's death, his brain was cut into 240 pieces and preserved for future study. Researchers think that Einstein was actually missing two pieces of brain anatomy that come standard with most brains. The lack of this standard equipment could have forced him to think in a unique way.

Einstein's brain also had more of the cells that provide nutrition to the brain than most people, particularly in an area of the brain that gathers information and puts it together in new ways.

Whether it was extra-special brain nutrition, a different way of thinking, or a combination of the two, there's no denying that Einstein was just a little more brilliant than the rest of us.

FACT

The Sky Is Not Blue

Let's say you could pick up the phone right now and get everyone on the planet (all seven billion of us) on the line at the same time. Call it a BIG conference call.

Then let's say you ask everybody to step outside and report on the color of the sky. Seems like a simple question. What would everybody say?

We're going to save you the trouble of making this call and cut straight to the answer. Since the weather around the globe, on average, is quite predictable, meteorologists have known the answer for a long time.

About 40% of the people will say "black" since it's night where they are. Another 35% will say "gray" or "brown" since it's rainy, overcast, dusky, morning, or smoggy for them. The smallest number, 25%, will say "blue". It doesn't matter when you place this call, the answer will always be the same. What does this mean? It means that the one single thing that you totally believed was 100% true isn't. We live on a planet where the sky is usually black or grey but for some reason nobody knows it.

25%
Blue

40% of
the time,
the sky
is Black

35%
Gray or
Brown

What color is the sky?

FACT

The Stars Are Not Countless

As long as we are on the topic of things you believe about the sky that aren't true, here's another one. The stars are not countless. Despite all the love songs and poetry, there actually aren't that many stars in the visible night sky. Even if you were in the desert on a clear night, there are only about 2,500 stars you can see, and if you wanted to, you could count them all in about a half hour.

Incidentally, this is one way we know that the universe isn't infinite and that it had a beginning. If the universe was infinitely big and if it had been around forever, there would be a star everywhere in the sky. In an infinite universe of countless stars, the sky would be completely, brilliantly, blankly white in every direction. And then you'd never get any sleep.

Bobby Leach (1858–1926)

 This Astounding Daredevil Was Killed by an Orange Peel

Since 1901, sixteen people have deliberately gone over Niagara Falls. Only eleven of those have survived the trip — and two of those went back for a second trip! But our favorite of all those was Bobby Leach (1858–1926), an astounding daredevil and a man whom we would instantly nominate for the Irony Hall of Fame.

In 1911, 53-year-old Leach became the first man to go over Niagara Falls in a barrel and survive. His barrel, 8 feet (2.4 m) long and pill-shaped, had been made for the purpose, and kept him safe through the harrowing trip — more or less. He emerged with a broken jaw and broken kneecaps. For the next fifteen years Leach had some success as a lecturer, describing his feat and displaying his battered barrel. His luck ran out when, while on tour in New Zealand, he slipped on an orange peel in the street, broke his leg, and died two months later of complications from the injury.

Leach was the first man to go over the falls, but not the first *person*. That honor goes to Annie Edson Taylor, a widowed school teacher who celebrated her 63rd birthday by going over the falls in a custom-made wooden barrel lined with mattresses and her lucky heart-shaped pillow. Taylor walked away with only a cut on her head, but

Annie Taylor, 1838–1921

she clearly hadn't enjoyed the trip. After they fished her out of the water, Mrs. Taylor is reported to have said "No one ever ought to do that again."

This Guy Farted for a Living

In the 1890s, Joseph Pujol (1857–1945) performed on stage with an act built around his amazing ability to control his farting. His stage name was *Le Petomane*, which roughly translates as "fartomaniac."

Pujol could play recognizable tunes, imitate thunder, and put out a candle at ten feet. For a time, he was the star attraction at the Moulin Rouge, a famous nightclub in Paris, where he played to packed houses.

In one incident, a woman in the audience became so overcome with hysterics that she fell out of her seat "and had to be carried out of the theatre by ushers for her own safety." Toward the end of his career, Pujol would end his act by performing his own version of the San Francisco Earthquake of 1906.

All this was made possible by Pujol's unique ability to control his abdominal muscles. His life inspired two musicals: *The Fartiste* (which won Best Musical at the 2006 New York International Fringe Festival) and *A Passing Wind,* which premiered at the Philadelphia International Festival of the Arts in 2011.

By the way, the term for someone who entertains an audience by farting in an amusing, creative, or musical way is *flatulist*. Not a word you're likely to use every day

...And This Guy Threw

Also known as "The Great Regurgitator" or "The 9th Wonder of the World," Hadji Ali (1888-1937) was a vaudeville sensation in the 1920s. In his act, he would swallow a wide range of objects that people generally avoid swallowing — like goldfish, watches, coins, jewelry, paper money, and pool balls. Then he would regurgitate them all in whatever order the audience demanded.

Ali was famous for his "human waterspout" routine. He drank two or three fishbowls of water, one cup after another. Then, with pinpoint accuracy, he vomited a stream of water into a basin waiting six feet away.

Up for a Living

His grand finale involved swallowing a large quantity of water, chased by a cup or two of kerosene. A small flame was set before him. With a blast of regurgitated kerosene, Hadji turned it into a roaring fire. Before the front row could panic, Hadji would put the fire out — by switching to regurgitated water. (We are not making this up. You can check it out on YouTube.)

But it gets even stranger. Hadji Ali was not the only guy of the time who made his living as a performing regurgitator. His competition included Harry "The Human Hydrant" Morton, and The Great Waldo, who, as part of his act, swallowed a locked padlock, then the key. He regurgitated the unlocked padlock.

Some Fossils Are Really Old Farts

Some 15 million years ago, a termite got caught in some sticky goo oozing out of a tree. The insect passed gas and died.

The goo hardened and fossilized around the dead termite, becoming the precious gemstone known as amber. Along with the insect, the amber preserved evidence of that cringe-worthy last moment. You see those bubbles? A poignant case of eternal embarrassment.

Termites, by the way, are chronic offenders in this area since they eat wood, which is tough to digest.

Since methane, the main gas in farts, contributes to global climate change, some have speculated that termites' noxious emissions contribute to this problem. Then again, so do the beans you ate for lunch.

Your Mother Wears Boiled Beetles

When fashion calls for screaming-red lipstick, the cochineal farmers of Mexico and South America get busy gathering beetles. That's because the bright red lips of fashion models are colored with carmine red (also known as crimson lake, or "natural red 4"). That's a dye made from the boiled innards of beetles known as cochineals.

To make a pound (about half a kilogram) of carmine red, you'd need about 70,000 cochineals. First, you drop the bugs into boiling water. Do not over boil. Then you dry the bugs thoroughly and crush them to powder. Boil the powder in ammonia, then strain out the crunchy bits. Dry the stuff again, and you'll end up with about a pound of dye.

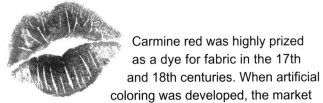

Carmine red was highly prized as a dye for fabric in the 17th and 18th centuries. When artificial coloring was developed, the market for carmine red dropped dramatically. But in the late 20th century, when several artificial red food colorings were found to cause cancer, carmine red, and the lowly cochineal, came back into style.

Today carmine red can be found in foods, drinks, candy, cookies, and cosmetics. But manufacturers go to great lengths to avoid telling the public where that luscious red color comes from... and it's probably just as well.

Sometimes it's better not to know about everything that's in your food.

Expensive perfumes are made with ambergris, which is basically sperm whale vomit.

Every box of cereal contains, on average, a few rat hairs.

Each cup of peanut butter includes, on average, about 60 tiny bits of insects.

FACT

You Will Sleep for 24 Years

Assume you're an average 12-year-old. You aren't, of course, but let's pretend.

- You will live to the age of 78 years, 11 months, and 13 days.

- You will watch TV for 8 years, 6 months, and 11 days.

- You will spend 11 years, 8 months, and 21 days surfing the internet.

- You will spend 3 years, 2 months, and 13 days in the bathroom.

And you will sleep for 24 years, 5 months, and 11 days. Although doctors would say another 3 years would make you feel better.

You'll spend more than three years here.

FACT

Sugar Does <u>Not</u> Cause Tooth Decay

No matter what your parents, teachers, and dentist have told you, sugar does not directly cause cavities.

But by the time you finish reading this page, you're going to wish it did.

Cavities are actually caused by acids produced by bacteria on your teeth. These bacteria eat food that's caught between your teeth — and sugar is one of their favorite foods. When bacteria digest sugar, they release acid as a waste product. That acid can dissolve a hole in the hard surface of your tooth, giving you a cavity.

So?

Bacteria are living organisms, just like you. And when you digest food and drink, you too produce a liquid waste product. (Hint: It's yellow).

You see where this is going? Sugars are not the direct cause of cavities. Neither are the bacteria that feed on sugars. Cavities come from the liquid that bacteria produce.

Bacteria have been peeing on this tooth.

That's right, gentle reader, here's the real reason your teeth are rotting. Sugar-loving bacteria in your mouth are peeing on them.

Right.

Now.

Making Your Bed Encourages These Hideous Vermin

The average human bed is home to anywhere between one and ten million dust mites, like the ones pictured here.

Not only do these critters look like something out of a horror movie, they can trigger asthma, eczema, and a condition called perennial rhinitis, which we won't talk about, but it's nasty. Dust mites love to bask in the warmth and moisture created by your sleeping body, and they feed on the thousands of skin flakes you shed every night. (Don't be self-conscious; it happens to the best of us). They also thrive in the unventilated, snug sheets you get when you make your bed really nice.

Over a million dust mites share your bed.

How can you make your home less welcoming to these tiny monsters? Simple. Do NOT make your bed.

Dr. Stephen Pretlove of London's Kingston University, an expert on dust mites, says that a messy bed, with the sheets just tossed aside and left as they fall, creates well-ventilated, dry conditions that cause mites to dehydrate and suffer a long, slow, painful death. (Actually, we just made up that part about the long and slow, but it does kill them.)

You may want to share this scientific information the next time someone suggests that you make your bed. Be sure to show the picture, too.

FACT

Toast Always Lands Butter-Side Down

As you know too well, if you accidentally knock a piece of toast off a table, it will land butter-side down.

This is not just because the universe is evil. Toast falling off a table picks up a spin. For most ordinary table heights, the toast has enough space to finish a half-flip right when it reaches the ground in a toasty belly-flop.

You could easily fix this problem by eating breakfast on a ladder. The extra height would allow enough space for the toast to make a full rotation and land butter-side up.

Alternatively, and maybe more conveniently, if everyone were twelve feet tall, tables would be higher. We'd be good. At least as far as falling toast is concerned.

Unfortunately, there's a problem with this solution. People that tall would frequently break their legs. They'd weigh roughly eight times as much as six-footers, but their legs would only be four times as strong. This is one reason why you never meet giants except in fairy tales.

Playing the Lottery Does Not Significantly Help You Win

FACT

The Mega Millions lottery jackpot is typically around $12 million. Say you caught a break and won it all. That would give you a daily $328.76, assuming you live another hundred years.

Not bad.

The odds aren't good — about one in 175 million — but what the heck. You can't win if you don't play, right? The people who run the lottery rely on that kind of thinking.

Here's another way of thinking about it: Winning the jackpot on a one-in-175-million shot is like reaching blindly into a jar of jelly beans, one white, the rest black, and coming out with the white.

Except it's not one jar, it's 388,000 jars. That's a large swimming pool full of jellybeans — and only one of them is white.

Your chances of guessing this man's full name are better than your chances of winning the lottery.

The decision to pay a dollar and dive blindfolded into a swimming pool for the white bean is not what mathematicians would call a "smart" thing to do. As you might suspect, your chances of getting that bean are small enough to disregard. In practical terms, they are zero, identical to what they were before you spent your dollar.

What's worse, your chances of winning don't go up the more you play. The same goes for any kind of gambling: whether it's the lottery, roulette, slot machines, or a simple coin flip, you're never "due for" a win. You can dive into that swimming pool over and over, but the beans are rearranged each time, so it doesn't matter. The only surefire way to win would be to buy 175 million tickets at once. And we're pretty sure they won't let you do that.

There is a ridiculously tiny chance that this monkey could randomly hit the computer keys in the right order to create a best-selling novel. But we wouldn't bet on it.

This Is the World's Ugliest Animal

This is a photo of the "eyelash mite" — a parasite that lives on your eyelashes and burrows into the pores that your eyelashes grow from. These mites are invisible to the naked eye, but you are looking at hundreds of them on the lashes of the nice lady pictured here. So you can appreciate the full-on ugliness of the mite, we've also included a closeup on the next page.

Almost everybody has eyelash mites. Yes, that's everybody — including you. You are home to a host of creatures. We're not just talking about fleas, ringworm, head lice, and bedbugs — which infest most of us from time to time but then (we hope) move on. We're talking about permanent parasites, the kind that never leave. As you read these words, you have about three pounds of bacteria living in your guts and on your skin.

You couldn't survive without them: some help you digest your food, and others fight off certain kinds of infections. Of course some of them do make you smell funny — body odor is a consequence of bacterial ooze.

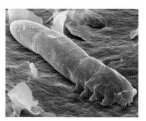

A closer view of the *Demodex* eyelash mite.

Humans, by the way, describe all the human parasites as ugly — whether they're leeches, ticks, or tapeworms. Generally, we seem to be prejudiced against the appearance of animals that suck our blood, poison us, or give us deadly diseases.

Completely icked out yet? Here's one very small fact to take comfort in: Though the eyelash mite spends all day feeding on the oil from your skin, it never poops.

⚜ A BEAUTY CONTEST ⚜
Squirrels vs. Rats

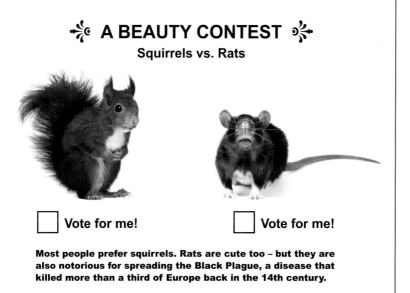

☐ Vote for me!   ☐ Vote for me!

Most people prefer squirrels. Rats are cute too – but they are also notorious for spreading the Black Plague, a disease that killed more than a third of Europe back in the 14th century.

The Universe Is Mostly Boring

Approximately 13.7 billion years ago, the universe was a very exciting place, full of enormous potential and occupying a space no bigger than this period.

And then — in an event that we feel safe in calling "epic" — the universe exploded and all the matter in it scattered. Among the many consequences of these events are peanut butter and jelly sandwiches, all 118 elements, black holes, billions of galaxies, and, of course, you.

All those things may sound interesting, but that stuff is insignificant compared to what you find in the rest of the universe. That is to say: Nothing. The vast majority of the universe is entirely empty — nothing is there. If the universe were reduced to the size of your hand, all the matter in it would occupy a space smaller than a hydrogen atom. The rest would be nothing.

Still think the universe is interesting?

Maybe you're thinking that the universe is empty, but our solar system is a happening place. So let's consider the solar system.

Suppose the sun is the size of a bowling ball. To find Neptune, you'd have to walk almost half a mile (about three-quarters of a kilometer), then look for something the size of a pea. Along the way, you'd probably miss the grains of sand that represented Earth, Venus, and Mars. Even Jupiter, the size of a marble, would be tough to find. Other than these small interruptions, we've got a whole lot of nothing.

You, like pretty much everything around you, are made of atoms. Do you know how empty those atoms are? If you could squeeze all the space out of all your atoms, you would be smaller than a grain of salt. Like the rest of the universe, you are filled with nothing.

Neptune is 2.8 billion miles (that's 4.5 billion km) from the sun. If the sun were the size of this picture of a bowling ball, and the pages of this book were laid out side by side, Neptune wouldn't show up until page 1,776 and it would be the size of this pea.

Sobering, isn't it?

Scientists say that things are happening in all the empty space that fills the universe — light is passing through and there's mysterious stuff called "dark matter." (Even scientists aren't sure what that is, though they're sure it exists.) But what interests us is how much of the universe has absolutely none of the matter that we think matters — the stuff that makes people and planets and peanut butter and jelly sandwiches. So by being boring and empty, the univese becomes interesting. Strange how that happens.

Maggots Are Your Friends

Leeches too. No, really.

During the Civil War, doctors noticed that wounded soldiers who were treated immediately sometimes did worse than soldiers left on the battlefield for days—even though the untreated wounds attracted flies and maggots.

The idea that a maggot-infested wound was less dangerous than a cleaned wound was disgusting. But the results were obvious: maggots could save your life.

When doctors began using antibiotics, the maggot "cure" was discarded. Not scientific. Not modern enough. Until doctors discovered that some wounds just don't respond to antibiotics. What to do?

Send in the maggots. "Medical grade" maggots (specially bred and sterilized) are used to clean out dead tissue in wounds that resist the usual treatments. Live tissue, you'll be happy to know, contains enzymes that maggots can't eat. Like a miniature clean-up crew, maggots clear out the garbage.

While we're on the subject of gross medicine, we can't resist mentioning leeches. For centuries, bloodletting — draining blood from a sick person — was standard practice. The idea was to get rid of the "bad blood" that made someone sick — either with a simple cut or with bloodsucking leeches. No telling how many people died as a result of this misbegotten theory.

Like maggots, bloodletting went out of style — until the 1980s, when a doctor discovered a modern use for leeches. A chemical in a leech's saliva stops blood from clotting. When a surgeon is reattaching an amputated limb, applying leeches can help keep blood flowing so tissue stays healthy. Gross, yes.
But very useful.

FACT

You Can Help Save the Universe by Leaving Your Socks on the Floor

Lots of kids don't like to pick up their socks or tidy their room. If that's how you feel, this is your page. Dr. Paul Doherty, chief scientist of San Francisco's Exploratorium, is happy to provide you with the perfect excuse to leave your room a mess.

Here's the excuse: Every time you clean your room you are speeding up the Heat Death of the Universe.

And here's Dr. Doherty's scientific explanation: Energy is always being transformed from one form into another. When a star explodes, stored energy in its nuclear core is converted into heat. When you bend down to pick up a sock, stored energy in your muscles is converted into heat.

And every time stored energy is turned into heat, the Heat Death of the Universe comes just a little bit closer.

As Dr. Doherty explains, the Heat Death of the Universe is when all available energy has been distributed evenly throughout the universe. Nothing is hot and nothing is cold. Everything is the same temperature.

When everything's the same temperature, you can't get any more work from heat moving from one place to another — and that's what runs our cars and factories. So everything grinds to a halt. When the Heat Death of the Universe is reached, there will be no light or life anywhere. Nothing but cold, lifeless rocks orbiting black, dead stars.

If that picture appeals to you, go ahead and pick up your socks. But if you want to help lengthen the life of our universe, do your part and leave them right where they are.

Do not move this sock. The universe depends on you.

Meteors Killed the Dinosaurs and a Dog

![FACT]

Not at the same time, of course.

In 1911, a man reported that a meteor struck and killed his dog in Nakhla, Egypt. Analysis of the meteorite* in the 1970s revealed that it came from Mars. Millions of years ago, a different meteor hit Mars and blasted pieces of the planet into outer space, launching one rock on a long flight path that eventually ended on a dog in Egypt.

This dog was not killed during an attack from Mars. But another one was.

The meteor that did in the dinosaurs slammed into Earth some 65 million years ago. The Chicxulub meteor, named for the Mexican village that's located in the center of the enormous crater it left behind, was about six miles wide. The energy of its impact was roughly 2 million times greater than the largest atomic bomb ever exploded. The resulting tsunamis, heat, fires, dust cover, acid rain, and shock wave wiped out virtually every

*Astronomers call a space rock a *meteor* when it's streaking through the atmosphere and a *meteorite* if it hits the ground.

species of animal on the planet larger than a house cat — including the dinosaurs.

Among the survivors were the mammals, a smallish collection of animals trying to get by in the shadow of the big guys, the reptilian dinosaurs. Since you and I are mammals, we take a more positive view of the Chicxulub meteor than do snakes and lizards today. And if it weren't for the Chicxulub meteor… you wouldn't be reading this book.

Miss Ann Hodges

On November 30, 1954 Ann Hodges of Sylacauga, Alabama was sitting in her living room when an 8 lb. meteorite came through her roof, bounced off the radio, and hit Ann in the thigh, raising a bruise. In all human history, this is the only documented case of a person being hit by a meteor.

Could a rock that size hit the Earth again? The answer,

The impact of the Chicxulub meteor left a crater that's 110 miles (over 100 km) wide.

you'll be sobered to learn, is "You betcha!" While we were working on this book, a meteor weighing more than 7,000 tons exploded over Russia, causing shock waves that broke thousands of windows. No one was killed, but it certainly took everyone by surprise.

Space scientists from around the world maintain a watch for incoming meteors, but they can only see the really big ones. So for all we know, a rock big enough to flatten a car could be headed your way… right… this… instant.

Cows Are Hazardous to the Environment

FACT

Poor cows. No one invites them to the movies. No one asks them over for a game of Monopoly. Aside from the obvious problem (they have no opposable thumbs), there's a very good reason to keep cows out of your living room: Cows produce methane.

As every chemist knows, methane is the main gas you pass when you pass gas. And cows pass a lot of gas. It doesn't matter what you feed Bossy. Grass, hay, grain — it all comes out the same. In the end, a by-product of a cow's digestion is methane, and lots of it. A single cow can produce more than 100 liters of the stuff a day — enough to empty a room.

"Who, me?"

All this gas-passing has consequences (other than making cows unpopular house guests). Methane, like carbon dioxide, is a "greenhouse gas," which contributes to global climate change and increases in extreme weather patterns.

In a single year, one cow produces 36,500 liters of methane. Multiply by 92.6 million cows in the U.S. alone and you get, well, a *lot* of gas*. Worldwide, one-and-a-half billion cows can — and have — altered the composition of the Earth's atmosphere.

* 3,379,900,000,000 liters in a year, from American cows alone.

This Chicken Lived for More Than a Year Without His Head

Next time your Dad accuses you of "running around like a chicken with its head cut off," tell him about "Miracle Mike," the rooster who lived for 18 months after he got the axe.

In September of 1945, farmer Lloyd Olsen chose Mike for Sunday dinner and chopped off his head with an axe. Ordinarily a beheaded chicken flaps around for a minute or so before keeling over. But Mike was no ordinary chicken. Despite his headless state, Mike hopped around, preened his feathers, and pecked at chicken feed with his now non-existent beak.

Mr. Olsen had the good sense to recognize Mike's remarkable achievement and brought the rest of the family (and soon neighbors and townsfolk) over to witness it. When a *Time* magazine article made Mike famous, the Olsens took him on the road, charging 25 cents a look. Soon "Mike, the Headless Chicken" was earning $4,000 a month.

The attention didn't go to Mike's head (of which he had none), but he did thrive, going from 2½ pounds at the time of his decapitation to a strapping 8 pounds. Mike's end came suddenly in a motel room in Phoenix, Arizona. The Olsens had forgotten the syringe they used to feed Mike at the sideshow and were helpless when he choked.

Feeding time

An autopsy revealed the secret to Mike's success. The axe that took off his head had not severed the main blood vessel to the head or the brain stem, which controls breathing and heart rate. If not for the accidental choking, Mike might have lived for quite a few more years.

Every year, Mike's home town of Fruita, Colorado, holds a festival in honor of Mike's will to live. Call it a celebration of the human — er, chicken — spirit.

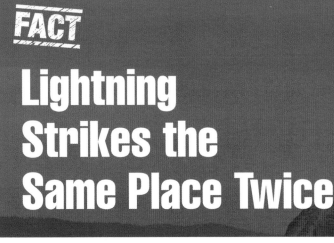

Lightning Strikes the Same Place Twice

The old saying "lightning never strikes in the same place twice" has got it exactly backward. On any given day, something like eight million lightning bolts strike the Earth, and they definitely have favorite targets. Isolated mountaintops all over the world bear the scars of millions of lightning strikes, and the Empire State Building gets hit about 100 times a year.

Why do those places attract lightning bolts? The National Weather Service says it's their height, pointy shape, and isolation from other tall pointy things. To avoid lightning bolts, you want to be shorter than the things around you, not too pointy, and not sticking out like a sore thumb.

Lightning is a form of static electricity, a giant version of the spark you sometimes get when you shuffle across a carpet, then touch a metal doorknob. In a thunderstorm,

Half Dome is a massive rock peak overlooking Yosemite Valley. It's a popular destination for hikers. And lightning.

a huge static charge builds up between the clouds and the ground. Scientists aren't exactly sure what creates the charge, but they know that lightning is a release of that charge. Electrically speaking, lightning relieves uncomfortable pressure. You could think of it as a planetary burp.

An "average" bolt of lightning carries a jolt of 200 million volts, which is why a direct hit by lightning is always fatal: People who survive lightning strikes are actually surviving near-hits.

Among near-strike survivors the world-record-holder is Park Ranger Roy Sullivan, who survived seven near-hits. "My friends would all leave me any time it started to cloud up…."

Roy Sullivan: Struck by lightning seven times

FACT

The Cockroach is Earth's Most Successful Animal

If aliens ever come to visit Earth they will probably name it Planet of the Beetles, since there are more beetles — and more species of beetles — than any other variety of animal. Cockroaches are one of the most successful branches of the beetle species (if you measure success by population count).

Common Roach (Rutilus rutilus)

The modern cockroach first appeared roughly 100 million years ago. Then, as now, cockroaches survived by scurrying out from underfoot (the feet at the time belonged to dinosaurs). A hundred thousand years ago, barely yesterday in cockroach time, a new predator species appeared that was wily, adaptable, and determined to use all means available to kill cockroaches — including chemical weapons of mass destruction. That would be us, *Homo sapiens*.

But despite our efforts to exterminate them, cockroaches thrive. Estimates are that there are ten cockroaches for every

Rescue Roach. Researchers have equipped roaches with cameras to investigate disaster sites.

human being on the planet, and nobody thinks that number is going anywhere but up. In fact, from the cockroach's point of view, humans have been very useful. We create cities that are a great place for roaches to live, providing safety from birds and other natural predators.

Here, in bulleted form, are a few of the reasons cockroaches do so well:

- A cockroach can go for weeks without food or water — and can live for weeks on the glue found on the backs of postage stamps.

- Thanks to the density of the atmosphere and the force of gravity here on Earth, a cockroach cannot fall to its death.

- A female of the most common species produces about 150 baby roaches over her 200-day lifespan.

- A cockroach can go for days without a head. (You try that sometime).

This Man Lived for a Dozen Years with a Hole in His Head

On September 13, 1848, Phineas Gage, a 25-year-old railroad construction foreman, was preparing to blast a section of rock wall near Cavendish, Vermont. Using a heavy iron rod, he was packing blasting powder into a deep hole bored into the rock, a job he had done many times before.

Then something went horribly wrong. The iron rod struck a spark and ignited the powder. The resulting explosion sent the iron rod through Gage's head, entering under the left cheekbone and exiting through the top of his head. The rod flew 25 yards beyond him. It was going that fast, with that much force.

One would expect the story — and Phineas — to end right there. But they did not. Gage not only survived the immediate incident, he was conscious and able to talk to a local physician, who wrote about Gage's head in a paragraph that still defies belief:

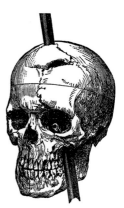

Although he survived the accident, it's hard to call the whole experience a "near miss."

> I first noticed the wound upon the head before I alighted from my carriage, the pulsations of the brain being very distinct. Mr. Gage, during the time I was examining this wound, was relating the manner in which he was injured to the bystanders. I did not believe Mr. Gage's statement at that time, but thought he was deceived. Mr. Gage persisted in saying that the bar went through his head...

You'd think a hole in your head would be a long-term medical problem, but over the next year Gage underwent a more or less complete recovery. He was well enough to travel, exhibiting his wound and the iron bar that caused it. He went on to spend seven years working in South America as a stagecoach driver. At 37, after a series of seizures, Gage died in San Francisco. His skull and the rod are still on display at the Warren Anatomical Museum in Boston, Massachusetts.

Truth Is Exactly as Strange as Fiction

In 1838 Edgar Allan Poe wrote his one and only novel (*The Narrative of Arthur Gordon Pym of Nantucket*), a complicated story that includes a shipwreck. In the novel a handful of sailors survive by clinging to the overturned ship's hull. After many dreadful days of hardship

**Edgar Allan Poe
1809–1849**

and hunger, the survivors draw straws, kill the loser, and eat him. Poe named the dinner, er, sailor "Richard Parker." The novel was fiction, of course, unlike the following story…

In 1884, nearly 50 years after Poe wrote his book and 35 years after his death, a British ship, the *Mignonette*, sank in a South Atlantic storm. Four survivors managed to get away in a lifeboat. As the days wore on, and starvation loomed, three of the sailors conspired to kill and eat one of their own. The three who survived were later tried and convicted of murder and cannibalism in a sensational English trial. The name of the unfortunate sailor who was eaten? Richard Parker.

THE ILLUSTRATED LONDON NEWS

REGISTERED AT THE GENERAL POST-OFFICE FOR TRANSMISSION ABROAD.

No. 2370.—VOL. LXXXV.   SATURDAY, SEPTEMBER 20, 1884.   WITH EXTRA SUPPLEMENT } SIXPENCE. By Post, 6½d.

THE LOSS OF THE YACHT MIGNONETTE.—FROM SKETCHES BY MR. EDWIN STEPHENS, THE MATE.

The way in which they stowed themselves in the dinghy.

Sailing before the wind: How the dinghy was managed during the last nine days.

How the dinghy was managed in the heavy weather: with the stern sheets up aft, and the "sea anchor," made of the water-breaker bed and the head-sheets grating.

Parasitic wasp

FACT

Bugs Are Not Nice to Each Other

With all the problems bugs have with fly swatters and bug-eating birds, you'd think they'd keep it friendly among themselves.

But you'd be wrong. Incredibly wrong. Bugs do super nasty things to each other.

Parasitic wasps inject their eggs into beetles. When the eggs hatch, the baby wasps eat the inside of the beetle and then burst out its back, like that scene in the movie *Alien*. The scientific term for the bug that gets eaten alive, by the ironic way, is "host."

Another bug, strepsiptera, looks like a gnat. During its very short lifespan (only a few hours long), the male flies frantically around looking for a female. The females are waiting, living inside of other bugs (who are alive and no doubt extremely unhappy with all of this) with just their heads sticking out. If the males are lucky enough to find a female, the babies will be born inside of the other bug, who will then, understandably, vomit them out.

Hairworm abandoning drowning cricket

Our last example, the nematomorph hairworm, has to be the creepiest. The tiny larva of this worm lives in water. It gets inside a cricket when the unsuspecting insect takes a drink. When the larva grows up, the worm seizes control of the cricket's brain (scientific term: "zombification") and forces it to hop into the nearest body of water, where it drowns. All so the hairworm can swim happily away.

If you are feeling ever-so-superior to those hapless crickets, you should know that human victims of the rabies virus go into an uncontrollable slobbering phase before they die. Why? Because the rabies virus says so. It exits the dying body via saliva, and keeps on spreading. Biologically speaking, the number one job of every life form on the planet is to reproduce itself, and most just don't care how much they inconvenience others to do so.

Rabies virus

This Turtle Can Breathe Through Its Rear End

Turtles usually breathe air, just like you do. And they do that through their noses.

But some species of turtles that live in the water have another way to get oxygen into their bodies (which is, after all, what breathing is all about). These turtles suck water in through their rear ends, remove oxygen from the water, then blow the water back out.

The champion in this regard is the Fitzroy River turtle of Queensland, Australia, shown here. Locals call it the "bum-breathing turtle," and biologists note that these turtles can pump water in and out at rates of 15 to 60 times per minute, expelling it with enough force to break the water's surface.

This picture is 2.5 million years old. It shows the Andromeda Galaxy, located two and a half million light years away.

Everything Is On Time Delay

FACT

Imagine you're in a crowded room. You exchange a meaningful glance with someone and feel an instant and powerful connection. You know the other person felt the same connection at the exact same moment.

Don't be so sure.

It takes time for light to travel across the room — about one nanosecond per foot of distance traveled. You see only when that light enters your eye. So you never see what's happening right now, you see what was happening when the light started its journey. You are always looking into the past.

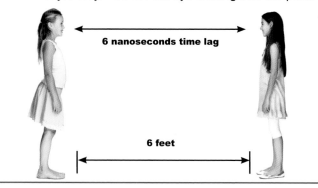

6 nanoseconds time lag

6 feet

Astronomers experience this problem far more acutely than lonely people in crowded rooms. At 93 million miles away, the sun is a vision from the past. Sunlight travels through empty space for 8.5 minutes en route to Earth. By the time you admire a lovely sunset, the show is over.

Pick any star in the night sky. It could have blown up years ago and you wouldn't know it. The light carrying that news is still on the way. From the very closest star to our solar system, light travels more than four years to reach Earth.

The entire night sky is a museum. With a good telescope you could look at starlight that left home before the dinosaurs were around — more than 65 million years ago.

Thinking about this leads to an interesting experiment. Suppose you're looking through a super-powerful telescope at a star 65 million light years away. It has a planet inhabited by super-intelligent aliens with telescopes. They are looking at our sun — our planet — at you — right now!

But the aliens aren't seeing you; they're seeing dinosaurs. The aliens that will see you will be born millions of years from now.

Knowing all of this, we suggest you hold up a big sign that says "Hello Aliens! I am an Earthling from the distant past. It's nice; wish you were here. Please hold up a sign and tell me what life is like where you are. I will leave word in my will for my descendants to look at you with their telescopes. Thank you."

Very pretty, but it's on an 8.5 minute time delay.

Mummy Brains Came Out Through Their Noses

A few years ago we created a list of *The Top Ten Coolest Things That Really Do Exist*. It's been helpful information for doing this book. On our list, the *Number Six Coolest Thing That Really Does Exist* is mummies.

Making a mummy is not as simple as wrapping a body in gauze and storing it for a long time. In ancient Egypt, making mummies was an entire industry with factories and thousands of mummy-making professionals. Why? Because it takes a lot of effort and all the Egyptians wanted to be one. A mummy, that is. For ancient Egyptians, regular everyday life was just a warm-up for the main event, which was life everlasting. To get to that eternal life, your body had to be preserved as a mummy.

We know about how the Egyptians made mummies because hieroglyphics and pictures show the steps, providing a "cookbook" for mummy-making. All the body's wet innards were removed and put into jars. Then the body was dried using heat and salts. Our favorite part of this recipe, one of the world's bigger yucks, is this: The brain was scooped out through the nose with a brain hook.

You might think that fishing for a person's brain through the nose would no longer be considered good medical practice. But neurosurgeons today still use the technique when they remove tumors from the brains of living people. The modern process is much more high-tech than the Egyptian brain hook, involving a tiny camera that helps surgeons see exactly what they need to remove.

The Tongue-Eating Louse Is the Grossest Creature on the Planet

We know that's quite a claim. But having reviewed many disgusting items for this project, we feel we are uniquely qualified to make this pronouncement.

Check out the tongue-eating louse (scientific name *Cymothoa exigua*) and we think you'll agree. It's small, not much longer than an inch when full grown, and lives throughout the eastern tropical and subtropical Pacific Ocean. A parasite, this crustacean lives inside fish, like the spotted rose snapper shown here. In its juvenile stage, the louse enters a host fish through the gills. Eventually the louse makes its way to the fish's tongue, where the parasite clamps on with its many claws and feeds on the fish's blood. All this blood sucking causes the tongue to wither, at which point the fish louse takes the place of the tongue. The fish, apparently, continues to feed and survive (although we have to wonder about what the fish thinks about all this).

Yuck.

In case you're wondering (and who wouldn't?) *your* tongue is safe: *Cymothoa exigua* doesn't go after humans. On the other hand, if you ever see one of these critters, don't pick it up — they bite.

One Cloud Weighs More Than Three Thousand 747s

We're talking about a cumulus cloud, one of those puffy white ones that look like piles of cotton. That cloud may look like a lightweight, but it's actually remarkably heavy.

Exactly how heavy? That depends on its altitude and temperature, but any average sized cumulus cloud contains a lot of water — hundreds of millions of gallons of water (or four times that many liters, if you like to measure things that way). If you've ever had to carry a bucket of water, you know that stuff is heavy.

No matter how light and puffy that cloud looks, it weighs more that 2.2 billion pounds (or a billion kilograms).

A Boeing 747 airliner, a commercial aircraft that can carry 400 people, weighs in at around 735,000 lbs (333,000 kilograms). It'll take more than 3,000 airliners to equal the weight of that one cloud.

What keeps all that weight up in the air? All the water in the cloud is in the form of tiny droplets. Those droplets are held up by the air. When one of these tiny droplets starts to fall, it bumps into air molecules and bounces around rather than falling. Of course, those tiny drops can join together to make big drops that are heavy enough to shove the air aside and fall down on your head as rain.

FACT

Cows Eat Magnets

Actual size

The object shown above is a magnet that a farmer will feed to a cow.

Yes, you read that right. A cow will eat that magnet. Why would a farmer feed a magnet to a cow?

Here's the punch line: So she doesn't get indigestion.

It turns out that cows aren't picky eaters. They'll eat all kinds of things that they shouldn't, including nails and barbed wire. It doesn't take medical training to realize that passing barbed wire through a cow's digestive system could end very badly.

This cow has a porthole. To understand how a cow's digestive system works, veterinary schools, and even some ranchers, have put windows into the sides of selected cows. Cannulated cows (as they are called) don't just survive the experience, they are frequently healthier than their windowless colleagues.

This specially designed magnet solves the problem. The magnet stays in the cow's stomach (or one of her stomachs — cows have four) and collects ingested metal, or "tramp iron" as it's poetically called. The resulting junkball stays put for the life of the cow, in a part of its digestive system where indigestibles get parked. We think that the farmer who thought of this — and the first cow to try it — both deserve a lot of credit.

There's a Word For "Big Rear End"

The English language got its start as a mash-up of a few Western European tongues, all of which are now defunct. But English, the mongrel child, has never been healthier. The number three language in the world, it's an evergreen, an open-source system, willing to take new words from anybody, anywhere, anytime. The result? A massive language with an enormous number of unique words for practically everything.

For proof, check out the Oxford English Dictionary (250,000 entries) or, if you're in more of a hurry, just look at "The Ten Coolest Words in the English Language You Probably Didn't Know," a list we have put together over a lifetime of study, and which we reprint here.

THE 10 COOLEST WORDS IN THE ENGLISH LANGUAGE YOU PROBABLY DIDN'T KNOW
(a connect-the-dots quiz)

CALIPYGIAN ● ● To go in a hurry

DEFENESTRATE ● ● Stuffed

ABSQUATULATE ● ● Ridiculous lies

HORNSWOGGLE ● ● Possessing a big rear end

BOBORYGMUS ● ● Toss out the window

PREPOSTEROUS ● ● The sound of a stomach rumbling

GALUMPHING ● ● Idiot

HOGWASH ● ● To fool

EXECRABLE ● ● Multi-syllabled; a fan of big words

NUMBSKULL ● ● Ridiculous

SESQUIPEDALIAN ● ● Stinky awful

FARCTATE ● ● Talk at great length about nothing

BLOVIATE ● ● Clomping around like a klutz

You'll find the answers in the dictionary (and on page 99.)

71

FACT

Columbus Did Not Discover America

In 1492, as we all know, Christopher Columbus sailed the ocean blue. That's true.

Most people also think Columbus discovered America on that trip — and that's just not so.

On that voyage, Columbus landed on an island in the Caribbean, claimed it for Spain, and called the people who lived on the island "Indians." After all, he figured he had reached the "Indies," as Asia was known at the time. That's where he was headed, after all.

This rather colossal misunderstanding began with a math problem. When planning his trip, Columbus confused two different measurements: the Arab mile and the Roman mile. (Back then, there were many different kinds of miles, each a different length.) As a result, Columbus underestimated the distance from Spain to the Indies.

The true distance was about 18,000 miles (the kind we're used to) or 29,000 kilometers. If Columbus had known that, he never would have left port. In 1492, no ship could carry enough food and water for such a long trip.

In any case, Columbus wasn't the first western explorer to find his way to the New World. In the 1960s, archeologists dug up the remains of a medieval Norse settlement built during the 10th century in northern Canada. A Norse explorer named Leif Ericson had beaten Columbus to the New World by nearly 500 years.

Columbus didn't know where he was and didn't know what he'd accomplished and he didn't do it first, but his timing was good. Word of his discovery spread quickly throughout Europe. Sometimes history favors the folks who know how to spread the news.

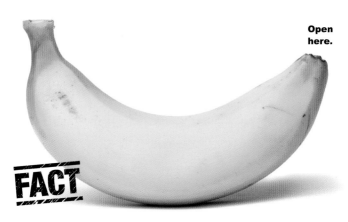

Open
here.

FACT

You Don't Know How to Peel a Banana

We once watched a chimp peel and eat a banana. Rather than starting at the stem, the chimp opened it at the other end.

Naturally, being open-minded human beings, our first thought was, "dumb ape." But in a rare moment of fairness, we decided to try it ourselves and discovered an amazing thing: it's actually easier to open a banana starting at the other end — especially with those annoying green bananas.

Lesson? Dumb human.

Why had we been peeling bananas the wrong way for years? Because long ago we told our brains the following rules: 1) Things open from the top, and 2) The stem is at the top.

So when we handed our brain a banana, it just followed the program. Find the stem; that's the top; peel from there. Rules like this keep things simple, and our brain likes that. It took a chimp to show us another way.

The expert

We didn't like where all of this was going, but then we went further. What other kinds of programming have we put into our brains to keep things simple (but wrong)? Deep stuff we're blind to? With consequences far more serious than banana damage? Could "stereotypes", "biases", and "prejudices" simply be bigger examples of "stuff opens from the top" programming?

Still more embarassing, in this case we didn't even get the "open at the top" part right. It turns out that bananas grow with the stem end closest to the ground and the other end curving upward.

Thomas Crapper Did Not Invent the Toilet FACT

Who invented the light bulb? How about the telephone? The flush toilet?

You probably said: Thomas Edison, Alexander Graham Bell, and Thomas Crapper.

Wrong. Each of these guys improved on work done by earlier inventors. At least 15 inventors (all un-famous) came up with (less practical) light bulbs before Edison. But Edison is the one we remember.

And everyone knows that Alexander Graham Bell invented the telephone, and that the first words spoken by phone were: "Watson! Come here."

But 16 years earlier a German inventor named Johann Philipp Reis beat Bell to the draw with a telephone prototype. The very first thing he said on the telephone was "Das Pferd frisst keinen Gurkensalat," which translates as "The horse doesn't eat cucumber salad." (We did not make that up.) Maybe Bell gets the credit because his phrase was catchier.

The truth about the inventor of the flush toilet makes us very sad. Thomas Crapper (1836 – 1910) was a real guy, the owner of a successful plumbing business in London toward the end of the 19th century. He did a great deal to popularize, improve, and repair the flush toilets that were being installed in all the modern buildings in London. But credit for the actual invention goes to an English nobleman, John Harrington, (1561–1612) who designed one for his godmother's bathroom (that would be Queen Elizabeth I).

Das Pferd frisst keinen Gurkensalat

Why do Edison, Bell, and Crapper get the glory while Reis, Harrington, and others are swept into History's broom closet? Good timing and one other thing: each of these gentlemen was persistent, always improving their work and keeping it (and their own names) in the public eye.

Vanity Made Pennies Worth $1000 Each

Of all the ways to make a lot of money, our favorite is just plain finding it. So much simpler than applying for a job (all those forms!) and it doesn't take a lifetime of drudgery (who has that kind of time?).

The ideal way to find money is to recognize that an object everyone else overlooked is actually a treasure. That brings us to the VDB penny, a rare and sought-after U.S. coin.

This is worth three dollars...

Take a close look at the picture so you'll be sure to recognize this penny if you're lucky enough to find one. Notice the year — 1909 — and the S below it, the mark of the San Francisco mint. But most important of all, check out the initials VDB at the edge of the coin. Those initials stand for Victor David Brenner, the Russian-born freelance designer of the coin.

The mint's staff designers didn't get to "sign" their work, and they raised a ruckus when they realized what Brenner had done. As a result, the initials were taken off the mold — but not before the pennies got into circulation.

Only 500,000 VDB pennies were minted in San Francisco. If you find one in good condition, it's worth a couple of thousand dollars.

A VDB penny without an S under the date was made in Philadelphia, where around 28 million VDB pennies were minted that year. In good condition it could fetch $15 or $20.

...and this is worth $1000.

FACT

A Blank Wall Was More Popular Than the Mona Lisa

In 1911, the Mona Lisa, regarded today as the world's most famous painting, was stolen from the world's largest and most famous art museum, the Louvre in Paris.

You might think that the museum would suffer without its star attraction — but you'd be wrong. Following the theft, the museum was closed for a week as detectives searched for clues. But when the Louvre reopened, people crowded in to see the empty space where the Mona Lisa had once hung — a blank spot on the wall marked with four iron pegs. That blank spot on the wall became the single biggest attraction in the museum.

While it was missing, the painting became a sensation. Photos of it appeared in newspapers around the world. Postcards picturing the painting sold everywhere. There were popular songs about the theft, and advertisements featuring the Mona Lisa's mysteriously smiling face.

It wasn't until 1913, when the painting was found and returned to the museum, that the crowds at the Louvre started thinning out and attendance returned to normal.

A Penny Thrown from the Empire State Building Will Not Kill You

The Empire State Building is 102 stories tall and over 1,400 feet high. It was built in 1931 and was the tallest building in the world for 40 years. In 1945 an airplane crashed into it. In 1979 a woman jumped from the 86th floor. The wind blew her back and she landed on the 85th. Every year a footrace is held from the bottom to the top. (Current record? Just over nine minutes. That's five and a half seconds per story.) And of course in 1933, a giant ape climbed to the top and was shot down by fighter planes.

Interesting stuff, but the question everyone always has is… what would happen if you dropped a penny off the top? If it hit someone, would it kill them?

Answer: No. Not even close. A penny falls more like a feather than a rock. It's so small and light that after 50 feet, it would be falling as fast as it could. If the air were perfectly still, the falling penny could reach a speed of 50 miles per hour (that's about 80 kilometers per hour). If you tried to catch it, it would sting your hand a bit, but nothing more. It wouldn't matter if the building were ten times taller. As long as there's air to slow the falling penny down, it won't go any faster.

However, if the Earth's atmosphere went away, the penny would continue accelerating all the way to the ground, where it could break bones in your hand. (Of course, you'd already be dead, having suffocated when the atmosphere vanished, so maybe a broken hand wouldn't bother you much.)

What would happen if you tried to catch a penny that was falling from the Empire State Building?

The Biggest Animal Ever Was Not A Dinosaur

FACT

There were some big dinosaurs — no question about that. In 1993, paleontologists found fossil remains of the one that's widely recognized as the reigning all-time heavyweight. The argentinosaurus is estimated to have reached lengths of 130 feet (about 40 meters) and tipped the scales at 220,000 pounds (about 100,000 kilograms).

It's a challenge to imagine what an animal that size looked like. An elephant is everybody's "big animal," but the largest elephant on record weighed 27,000 pounds (about 12,000 kilograms). An argentinosaurus weighed 8 times that. Think of a locomotive with legs. Or consider a dino-pie the size of a single bed. Since these plant-eating dinosaurs would probably travel together, you really should think of a stampeding herd of argentinosauri.

When you're done doing all of that, then it's time to close your eyes and imagine an animal that weighs twice as much as an argentinosaurus. That's an animal that's still around. It's called a blue whale.

By weight, the blue whale is the largest animal ever known to have existed. Ever. Individuals have been reliably measured at 100 feet (30.5 m) in length and 400,000 pounds (181,000 kg), if that makes it any easier to imagine. It's big enough to give you and 200 friends a ride. It has a heart the size of a Volkswagen and eats 7,900 tons of plankton a day. With all due respect to the dinosaurs, even the biggest would be nothing but a weenieosaurus next to our own blue whale.

Elephant

Argentinosaurus

Not shown actual size.

Thanks to Sword Swallowers, Doctors Can See Inside You

FACT

Sword swallowing is an ancient practice — it started in India around 4,000 years ago. Its history includes a grim chapter during the Spanish Inquisition when sword swallowers were deemed to be practitioners of a dark art and were put to death.

But sword swallowing isn't magic and it isn't an optical illusion. A sword swallower tips his head back and runs a sword all the way down his throat into his stomach — a very tricky and dangerous activity. Don't try this at home (or anywhere else). Mastering it takes more than 5 years of practice and very steady nerves. Sword swallowers must relax the muscles involved in swallowing, something most people can't consciously do. They also have to control their gag reflex, a natural defense against choking that's activated when something touches the back of the mouth.

Back in 1868, a German doctor named Adolf Kussmaul realized that a sword swallower's amazing control could give him a peek inside a living human. Kussmaul designed a new medical instrument — a rigid 18-inch stainless steel tube lit up with an alcohol-turpentine lamp. The sword swallower inserted the tube down his throat (just like a sword, but not as sharp), and Kussmaul took a look inside the man's stomach, making medical history. Kussmaul's device was called an endoscope. Today, doctors use flexible endoscopes and cameras to inspect people's bodies from the inside out — thanks to a sword swallower whose name is long since forgotten.

Laughter Can Be Deadly

Is it possible to have too much of a good thing? It seems so. Death-by-Laughter (or Fatal Hilarity, as it is sometimes known) has occurred throughout history, striking kings (King Martin of Aragon, 1410), philosophers (Chryssipus of Greece, 206 BC), and aristocrats (Sir Thomas Urquart, 1660).

In modern times, fatal hilarity has taken out less exalted folks. In March, 1975, Alex Mitchell, a bricklayer from Kings Lynn, England, was watching The Goodies, a British television comedy. In this episode an actor dressed as a Scotsman in a kilt attempted to beat back a crazed black pudding with a set of bagpipes in a demonstration of the Scottish martial art "Hoots-Toot-O-Chay." This struck Mr. Mitchell as overwhelmingly funny. After 25 minutes of helpless laughter he slumped to his couch, a victim of heart failure.

His wife later wrote the producers and thanked them for making her husband's last minutes on earth so pleasant. (You can watch the deadly episode on YouTube. Search "The Goodies, Kung-Fu Kapers." But do so at your own risk. You have been warned.)

FACT

Booth Saved Lincoln

As anyone who has studied American history knows, John Wilkes Booth shot and killed President Abraham Lincoln in 1865. But that's just part of the story.

In 1864, while on vacation from Harvard, Abraham Lincoln's oldest son, Robert, was waiting on a train platform in Jersey City, New Jersey. The platform was crowded, and young Lincoln was accidentally pushed into the gap between the train and platform. Before he could be hurt or killed, a nearby stranger leapt to his aid and pulled him to safety.

Robert's rescuer was Edwin Booth, one of the great actors of the time. Only a few months later John Wilkes Booth,

Robert Lincoln, 1843–1926

Edwin's younger brother, would become infamous as the man who assassinated Robert Lincoln's father.

Robert Lincoln went on to a long career in politics and law, serving as Secretary of War under President Garfield and Ambassador to England under President Harrison. But he seemed to be bad luck for American presidents. In all of American history, there have been four presidential assassinations and Robert Lincoln was present at three of them: Lincoln in 1865, Garfield in 1881, and McKinley in 1901. Robert Lincoln was aware of and disturbed by this coincidence. After McKinley's death, he turned down most presidential invitations, commenting "there is a certain fatality about presidential functions when I am present."

Edwin Booth, 1833–1893

There Are Dead Vikings In Your Drinking Water

FACT

Although planet Earth is a very big place, it is not an open system. There are no new shipments of water or air arriving from outer space. The proportions of the mix have changed, but if you weighed the planet a billion years ago and then again today, the weight would be roughly the same.

That's why people talk about conserving resources all the time. It would be nicer if there were pickups and deliveries from galactic trucks, but we're stuck. We have to deal.

Take a deep breath and hold it while we tell you that you are not the first to use this air. Many others have used it. Millions, in fact. It's very likely that some tiny bit of the air in every breath you take was also in the lungs of Julius Caesar at the moment he died.

To figure that out, we did the math. The air in your lungs is made up of molecules, the tiny bits that make up everything in the world. The number of molecules in a single breath is a ridiculously big number — written as 1 with 22 zeros after it. A billion is a 1 with 9 zeros after it, and a trillion is a 1 with 12 zeros after it. This ridiculously big number is equal to 10 billion times a trillion. If you want a name that doesn't involve so many zeros, you could call it 10 sextillion, but we'll just stick to calling it ridiculously big.

In the two thousand years since Caesar perished, that ridiculously big number of molecules from his last lungful have scattered uniformly throughout the Earth's atmosphere — and the odds are very good that every breath you take contains a molecule of that air.

The same principle applies to water. Because the human body is about 75% water, it's almost certain that every glass you drink contains water molecules that were part of a brave Viking who died a thousand years ago. And many millions of years ago, some dinosaur drank that water and…well you know what happens eventually to water after you drink it.

This man is drinking dinosaur pee.

This Is the Deadliest Animal of All

FACT

The female *Anopheles* mosquito has killed more humans than any other animal. By far.

You can talk all you want about sharks, crocs, grizzlies, and various vipers, but when it comes to animals and human slaughter, there is only one Death Animal; everybody else is laughable.

Meet the female *Anopheles** mosquito. In the time it takes you to read this page, she will claim another victim — probably a child. Over the last 100,000 years — call that the history of humanity — she has killed billions (that's *billions*, with a "b"). The World Health Organization estimates that half (half!) of the human race is at risk of dying from the bite of the female *Anopheles* mosquito and the infection she carries.

The familiar name of the infection is malaria, and the scientific name is *Plasmodium*. It's a parasite, a single-celled protozoa, and it invades healthy cells and destroys them. Fifty thousand could swim in a pool of blood the size of this period. But it takes only one to do the job.

The word Anopheles *is Greek for "useless."*

You Are Related to *Everyone* Ever

You are related to the lady in line at the grocery store ahead of you. You are also related to A-Rod, Bozo the Clown, Lady Gaga, Albert Einstein, Kanye West, and your third grade teacher. The reason? You're a member of the human race and we are family.

Take a look at your family tree. If you go back one generation, you have your parents. That's two people. Go back another generation to your grandparents, and that's four people. By the third generation you've got eight people —

your great-grandparents. By the time you go 40 generations (about 1,000 years) back, you have one trillion ancestors. That's more than all the people who have ever lived. Which means that some of your ancestors were already related. The mathematics are mind-boggling.

If you want to get even more excited, this means you are related to a whole lot of kings and queens and emperors and world conquerers — like Julius Caesar, Ghengis Khan, Charlemagne, the Chinese Emperor Gaozu, Queen Victoria, and Hannibal. You might mention that next time you're not getting the kind of respect someone with royal blood deserves.

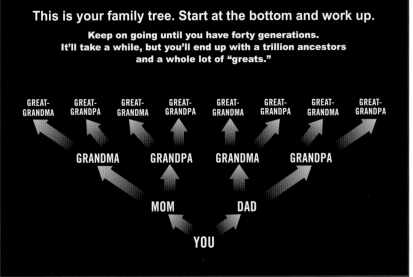

This is your family tree. Start at the bottom and work up.

**Keep on going until you have forty generations.
It'll take a while, but you'll end up with a trillion ancestors
and a whole lot of "greats."**

GREAT-GRANDMA GREAT-GRANDPA GREAT-GRANDMA GREAT-GRANDPA GREAT-GRANDMA GREAT-GRANDPA GREAT-GRANDMA GREAT-GRANDPA

GRANDMA GRANDPA GRANDMA GRANDPA

MOM DAD

YOU

Acknowledgments

Head Know-It-All................John Cassidy

Editor ....Pat Murphy

Design.................................Kevin Plottner

Science Advisor.................Paul Doherty

Art Direction.......................Jill Turney

Production..........................DeWitt Durham, Kelly Shaffer,
Linda Olbourne

Production Editor. ....Madeleine Robins

Assistant Know-It-Alls ......Nicholas Berger, Dan Letchworth,
Madeleine Robins

Editorial Assistance ....Rebekah Lovato Piatte, Dan Letchworth

Models

Patrick McEntee, Ryan Traynor,
Wolfe Price

Photo Credits

Cover top: thinkstock; cover bottom left: Dr. Gregory S. Paulson, Shippensburg University; Cover bottom right: Wikimedia; left: Antonio Petrone/Shutterstock; right: Wikimedia. Page 1: Dreamstime. Page 2: top, Shutterstock; bottom, Dreamstime. Page 3: top, Bob Carey/Media Bakery; bottom, Dreamstime. Page 6: Dreamstime. Page 7: Thinkstock. Page 9: Tom Collicott/Masterfile. Page 10–11: RT Images/Shutterstock. Page 11: inset, Dreamstime. Page 12–13: Peresanz/Shutterstock. Page 14: © Buffalo History Museum, used by permission. Page 15: The Granger Collection, NYC. Page 16: Pujol, Wikimedia; frame, iStockphoto; cloud, Thinkstock. Page 18–19: National Photo Company Collection/LOC/Wikimedia. Page 20–21: Mark Thiessen/National Geographic Stock. Page 22: Zyance/ Wikimedia. Page 23: Dreamstime. Page 24: ImagesEurope / Alamy. Page 25: bottom right, Dreamstime. Page 26: Classic Stock/Superstock. Page 27: iStockphoto. Page 28–29: Shutterstock. Page 31: Dreamstime. Page 32: Peter Fox. Page 33: top, Old Visuals/Alamy; bottom, Morgan Lane Photography/Alamy. Page 34: Image Source/Alamy. Page 35: top, Andrew Syred/Science Source; bottom left, Life on white/Alamy; bottom right, Shutterstock. Page 36: Dreamstime. Page 38: Chris Barber/Alamy. Page 39: shutterstock. Page 40: Peter Fox. Page 41–42: Dreamstime. Page 43: top, University of Alabama Museums; bottom: Shutterstock. Page 44: shutterstock. Page 45: Dreamstime. Page 46–47: Bob Landry/Time & Life Pictures/Getty Images. Page 48–49: top, Courtesy of M. Bruce MacIver, Stanford University. Page 49: bottom, AP Photo. Page 50: Dreamstime. Page 51: top, Katsumi Kasahara/AP Photo; bottom, Shutterstock. Page 52: portrait, Wikimedia; frame, Dreamstime. Page 53: Wikimedia. Page 54: Library of Congress/LC-USZ62-10610.

Page 55: TopFoto/The Image Works. Page 56: Dr. Gregory S. Paulson, Shippensburg University. Page 57: top, D. Andreas Schmidt-Rhaesa/Wikimedia; bottom, Chris Bjornberg/Science Source. Page 58–59: Ken Griffiths/NHPA/Photoshot. Page 60: top, Robert Gendler; bottom. Page 61: Dreamstime. Page 62–63: ED/DW/Camera Press/Redux. Page 64–65: background, Dreamstime. Page 65: fish, Matthew R. Gilligan. Page 66–67 background, Thinkstock. Page 68: Courtesy of Master Magnetics, Inc. Page 69: Spectrum Photofile. Page 70: Dreamstime. Page 72–73: Shutterstock. Page 74: Dreamstime. Page 75: Thinkstock. Page 76: Hein Nouwens/Shutterstock. Page 77: DPA/Corbis. Page 78: Thinkstock. Page 79: iStockphoto. Page 80: Stuart Dee/Photographer's Choice/Getty Images. Page 81: Mary Evans Picture Library/Alamy. Page 82–83: Dreamstime. Page 84–85: background, Mark Conlin/Alamy. Page 85: top, Morphart/Can Stock Photo Inc.; bottom, Shutterstock. Page 86: Sword Swallower Dan Meyer. Page 87, 88, 89: Shutterstock. Page 90: Library of Congress. Page 91: Redferns/Getty Images. Page 92: Bob Carey/Media Bakery. Page 93: Dreamstime. Page 94: shark, Pacific Stock/SuperStock. Page 94: inset, Dreamstime. Page 96: Thinkstock. Page 99: Peter Fox.

Answers from p. 71

Calipygian	Possessing a big rear end
Defenestrate	Toss out the window
Absquatulate	To go in a hurry
Hornswoggle	To fool
Boborygmus	The sound of a stomach rumbling
Preposterous	Ridiculous
Galumphing	Clomping around like a klutz
Hogwash	Ridiculous lies
Execrable	Stinky awful
Numbskull	Idiot
Sesquipedalian	Multi-syllabled; a fan of big words
Farctate	Stuffed
Bloviate	Talk at great length about nothing

What Do *You* Think?

The facts in this book were the greatest in history at the time we wrote this book. (At least, that's our opinion on the matter.) But maybe you think some are greater than others. Or you wonder about the accuracy of one of our facts. We invite you to be a fact-checker: Get online or open a book and see what you can find out. If you have questions, comments, or corrections, email us at thefolks@klutz.com. We welcome your thoughts and look forward to hearing from you.

MAIL-IN REBATE

NOT PAYABLE AT RETAIL

TO RECEIVE YOUR MAIL-IN REBATE CHECK YOU MUST:

❶ Purchase ONE (1) new copy of the full version of *The Encyclopedia of Immaturity, The Encyclopedia of Immaturity Volume 2,* and/or *The Klutz Book of Inventions*. (This offer does not apply to the Scholastic Book Clubs editions of these books, to *The Encyclopedia of Immaturity — Short Attention Span Edition*, or to *The Klutz Book of Inventions — Hall of Fame Edition*.) You will receive a rebate of $3 for each qualifying title you buy.

❷ Mail your original register receipt for the above book(s) along with this completed rebate form (not a copy) to:

"The World According to Klutz Offer"
c/o Klutz, 450 Lambert Avenue
Palo Alto, CA 94306

NOTE: REBATE OFFER VALID ONLY ON PURCHASES MADE AFTER JULY 1, 2013,
AND ALL REBATE REQUESTS MUST BE POSTMARKED BY
DECEMBER 31, 2015 AND RECEIVED BY JANUARY 31, 2016.

Rebate check should be made payable to:

Name: _____

Address: _____

City: _____

State/Province/Territory: _____ Zip Code/Postal Code: _____

Email (optional): _____ U.S.   Canada   (circle one)

To receive the full $9 in rebates, you must buy one copy of each title.
What did you buy?

❑ *The Encyclopedia of Immaturity*
❑ *The Encyclopedia of Immaturity Volume 2*
❑ *The Klutz Book of Inventions*